D1256802

BULLDOG BAD BOYS

BULLDOG BAD BOYS

And Some Pretty Uncontrolabull Girls, Too!

■ WILLOW CREEK PRESS

Published by Willow Creek Press
P.O. Box 147, Minocqua, Wisconsin 54548

Photo Credits:
p2 ©Tara Gregg/Sporthorse Photography; p6 ©Ron Kimball/Kimball Stock;
p9 ©Close Encounters of the Fury Kind/Kimball Stock; p10 ©Ron Kimball/Kimball Stock;
p13 ©Mark McQueen/Kimball Stock; p14 ©Richard Stacks/Kimball Stock;
p17,18,21 ©Ron Kimball/Kimball Stock; p25 ©Dave Blackey/agefotostock.com;
p26 ©Daniel Johnson/Paulette Johnson; p30 ©Renee Stockdale/Kimball Stock;
p33 ©Martin Rogers/Kimball Stock; p34 ©Richard Stacks/Kimball Stock;
p37 Johan De Meester/ardea.com; p38 ©Richard Stacks/Kimball Stock;
p41,42 ©Ron Kimball/Kimball Stock; p45 ©Tara Gregg/Sporthorse Photography;
p49 ©Renee Stockdale/Kimball Stock; p57 ©Mark McQueen/Kimball Stock;
p58 ©Ron Kimball/Kimball Stock; p61 ©Richard Stacks/Kimball Stock;
p62,65 ©Ron Kimball/Kimball Stock; p69 ©Tara Gregg/Sporthorse Photography;
p70,73 ©Ron Kimball/Kimball Stock; p74 ©Daniel Johnson/Paulette Johnson; p77 ©Jean M. Fogle;
p78 ©Tara Gregg/Sporthorse Photography; p82 ©Ron Kimball/Kimball Stock;
p85 ©Mauricio Ramos/agefotostock.com; p86 Johan De Meester/ardea.com;
p89 ©Corbis/agefotostock.com; p90 ©Ron Kimball/Kimball Stock; p93 ©Jean M. Fogle

Design: Donnie Rubo
Printed in Canada

BULLDOG LOVERS
BEWARE

Bulldogs are not necessarily the adorable little pooches they appear to be. This book, by way of example and in the spirit of public service, illustrates the nefarious characteristics typically displayed by this peculiar breed. Obtained from canine crime records throughout the land, the following reports represent a laundry list ranging from serious felonies to minor misdemeanors. Be on the lookout for such suspicious bulldog behavior in and around your residence.

NAME: FELIX
HEIGHT: 18"
WEIGHT: 63 LBS.

CHARGE: KIDNAPPING
Class I felony

When neighbors discovered their kitten had gone missing, suspicion immediately fell upon the next door bulldog, aka Felix, who had previously displayed unusual fondness for and attention to the victim. Acting on a hunch, investigators found both Felix and the kitten in the perpetrators home. The victim was rescued without further incident.

NAME: WINSTON
HEIGHT: 22"
WEIGHT: 58 LBS.

CHARGE: COERCION
Class II misdemeanor

Winston is a shameless and habitual seeker of belly
scratches from family members and their friends. His M.O.
is well-known: Advance toward the chosen victim with
wagging tail followed by a sudden, well-practiced roll
to his back that exposes his adorable pink belly.
If this fails to induce the desired scratch, he waggles
his front paws in the air until the victim succumbs.

CHARGE: GANG BANGING
Class III felony

This litter has in a short time become notorious for riotous behavior and malicious mischief both in and around the home. Criminal allegations include ankle biting, carpet wetting, gnawing on table legs, paper shredding, and general public disturbance. Authorities strongly suggest breaking up the gang after seven weeks and dispersing the pups to new homes where rehabilitation remains a possibility.

NAME: ANNIE
HEIGHT: 24"
WEIGHT: 81 LBS.

CHARGE: FELONIOUS CUTENESS
Class III misdemeanor

Annie is a three-year-old bulldog with a heart-warming smile and no fear to use it in illicit pursuit of various scams that include begging treats and family forgiveness for transgressions, i.e. mistakes on the carpet. Charges have been repeatedly dropped and the criminal remains at large.

NAME: BUSTER
HEIGHT: 13"
WEIGHT: 19 LBS.

CHARGE: EVADING AUTHORITIES
Class II misdemeanor

Family authorities were advised to be on the lookout
for Buster after he was released from the house to the
backyard with terms that he would return on his own
recognizance after doing his duty. When Buster failed to
appear within an appropriate time, investigators mounted
a search and discovered the malefactor hiding in a
basket. The dog remains under temporary house arrest.

NAME: PEARL
HEIGHT: 20"
WEIGHT: 82 LBS.

CHARGE: PUBLIC INTOXICATION
Class III misdemeanor

Pearl, unaware that the liquid spilled on the kitchen tile was a vodka martini, licked every last drop before embarrassing herself at her master's dinner party. Several incidents of misbehavior, including upsetting the appetizer platter and jumping on laps, were reported by guests. Pearl was sentenced to a St. Bernard-sized hangover.

NAME: MIKEY
HEIGHT: 19"
WEIGHT: 73 LBS.

CHARGE: FLEEING THE SCENE OF AN ACCIDENT

Class I misdemeanor

After knowingly and willingly entering a yard not his own, Mikey failed to resist the sudden urge to relieve himself. The perpetrator was observed in the act of the crime by a member of the Neighborhood Watch team who responded by yelling at the bulldog from her doorway and filing a telephone complaint to his owners. Mikey fled the scene of the accident but was quickly apprehended at home where charges are pending.

NAME: MIMI
HEIGHT: 21"
WEIGHT: 53 LBS.

CHARGE: CONTRIBUTING TO THE DELINQUINCY OF A MINOR

Class II misdemeanor

Mimi is a four-year-old bulldog and companion of three-month-old bulldog Daisy, only a recent member of the household. Although Mimi is fully trained and understands that the beds are strictly off limits, she has nonetheless been frequently observed and punished for lying on them. To compound this illegal behavior, she has encouraged Daisy to join in these crimes. Authorities are withholding treats for one week.

NAME: DUKE
HEIGHT: 22"
WEIGHT: 94 LBS.

CHARGE: ABSENT WITHOUT LEAVE
Class III felony

Duke is the mascot of the 12th Regiment, 5th Division of the U.S. Marine Corps. Discovered absent from his barracks, military police mounted an investigation leading to the apprehension of the wayward bulldog who was found accompanying a female Pomeranian visiting the base. After a brief tribunal leading to conviction, the unrepentant Duke was sentenced to post three hours sentry duty.

NAME: PUCK
HEIGHT: 27"
WEIGHT: 103 LBS.

CHARGE: DAMAGE TO A MOTOR VEHICLE
Class II misdemeanor

Apparently indignant at being left in the truck while his owner shopped in the pet store, Puck turned his toothy ire on the vehicles leather seat covers. Upon the owners return Puck was immediately contrite having sensed the enormity of his crime. His remorse, however, was deemed insufficient in and of itself and the bulldog was sentenced to immediate corporal punishment.

NAME: TANYA
HEIGHT: 20"
WEIGHT: 89 LBS.

CHARGE: ACCEPTING A BRIBE
Class III misdemeanor

Disinclined to ingest her pills by legal means, Tanya induced her owner to bribery using a meat scrap as the payoff. The suspect has been under surveillance for weeks and authorities are convinced they have an open and shut case.

NAME: TEENCEE
HEIGHT: 16"
WEIGHT: 67 LBS.

CHARGE: FELONY THEFT
Class II felony

Teencee is a three-year-old bulldog who should certainly know better. Nevertheless, when temptation presented itself at the backyard barbeque a previously undiscovered evil side overruled her good sense and she seized a string of frankfurters. After a hot pursuit at speeds up to four miles per hour, Teencee was seized by authorities and forced to surrender what remained of the stolen goods.

NAME: CHESTER
HEIGHT: 17"
WEIGHT: 49 LBS.

CHARGE: BIGAMY
Class I misdemeanor

Charges were filed against Chester who allegedly pledged his devotion (and a Pupperoni) to Maggie in exchange for a brief dalliance. Following consummation, Maggie learned that Chester was also engaged in a trysting relationship with Dora, a female Shih Tzu residing two blocks away. Maggie has separated from Chester and retains the Pupperoni.

NAME: FINNEGAN
HEIGHT: 25"
WEIGHT: 74 LBS.

CHARGE: MANSLAUBER
Class III misdemeanor

Finnegan was charged with sneezing and drooling at and upon her master's house guest. After being administered a tissue paper facial, suspect was mildly scolded. When the victim expressed a desire for leniency, charges were dropped and Finnegan was released upon his own recognizance.

NAME: REGGIE
HEIGHT: 23"
WEIGHT: 87 LBS.

CHARGE: STALKING
Class II misdemeanor

Reggie is currently under questioning by authorities
after numerous complaints from guests attending a
barbecue in the backyard of Keith and Helen Henderson
stating that the four-year-old bulldog continually
approached and lingered around the diners in a
suspicious manner. "He'd just stand there looking
at you, hoping for something to fall off your plate,"
stated one witness. "It was just plain eerie."

NAME: CATO
HEIGHT: 29"
WEIGHT: 110 LBS.

CHARGE: INTIMIDATION
Class III misdemeanor

His diminutive size notwithstanding, Cato is a ferocious defender of the front gate of his home—so much so that uniformed representatives of the U.S. Postal Service have advised his owners that mail delivery will be halted unless action is taken. As a result, Cato has been relieved from further duty and is reassigned to security issues within the household.

NAME: OTTO
HEIGHT: 25"
WEIGHT: 97 LBS.

CHARGE: OBSTINANCE
Class II misdemeanor

Following a string of incidences during which he was difficult to manage and control, Otto was reported to authorities. "He simply refuses to come when he's called," stated owner Nancy Ferguson in her complaint. "He just stands there and stares with a 'Make me' kind of look on his face." As a result of the incident, Otto has been fitted with a leash and will be monitored, and his outdoor activities will be closely supervised.

NAME: WILLY
HEIGHT: 22"
WEIGHT: 65 LBS.

**CHARGE: INDECENT EXPOSURE:
URINATING IN PUBLIC
(THIRD OFFENSE)**

Class III felony

Willy is a chronic public piddler who has tried and defied his neighborhood's patience and goodwill. Although this is his third arrest, forensic evidence found upon area lawns suggests Willy may be guilty of considerably more transgressions. Should further investigation lead to charges, Willy could be tried as a serial piddler, a Class II felony.

NAME: SANDY
HEIGHT: 12"
WEIGHT: 17 LBS.

CHARGE: INDOLENCE: FAILURE TO PLAY
Class III misdemeanor

Sandy is a seven-week-old bulldog puppy who reportedly sleeps up to 12 hours daily, a fact which greatly disappoints the Anderson's six-year-old daughter, Lauren, who wishes to play with her. The pup has been given a two month probation after which time it is expected her activity level will delight Lauren and overwhelm the parents.

NAME: CARTER
HEIGHT: 29"
WEIGHT: 89 LBS.

CHARGE: FUGITIVE FLIGHT
Class II felony

While secured and being escorted by a leash from his household to the public park, Carter broke from his master and fled for two hundred yards and was found hiding in a lilac bush. The dog gave up passively and the walk continued without further incident.

NAME: FRANCIS
HEIGHT: 25"
WEIGHT: 91 LBS.

CHARGE: BALL HOG
Class III misdemeanor

Francis is a habitual ball hog who obstructs the play of the household children. Although willing to retrieve, he willfully refuses to drop. His reluctance to share has led to home confinement with future charges pending.

NAME: BUSTER
HEIGHT: 29"
WEIGHT: 104 LBS.

CHARGE: PUBLIC NUISANCE:
OFFENSIVE ODER

Class II misdemeanor

Buster entered his residence via the back door presumably after doing his duty. It was immediately apparent to his owners, however, that the four-year-old bulldog had also willfully rolled in foul-smelling matter of his own making. Buster was quickly apprehended and sentenced to a detoxification facility followed by a night in the family garage.

NAME: MAX
HEIGHT: 19"
WEIGHT: 59 LBS.

CHARGE: INCITING A RIOT
Class III felony

Max (aka "Maxie") was charged with inciting a riot
in a public park. The incident occurred after the
short-legged Max was repeatedly confounded in his
attempts to retrieve a throw toy by a swifter dog
that authorities have yet to identify. Eyewitnesses
state that Max, frustrated by his failures, finally
ambushed and assailed the unknown dog, separating it
from the throw toy and causing it to flee the park.
The victim has not yet come forward to press charges.

NAME: KIKI
HEIGHT: 23"
WEIGHT: 60 LBS.

CHARGE: PUBLIC FLATULENCE WITH MALICE AFORETHOUGHT

Class I misdemeanor

Kiki, an eight-year-old bulldog, enjoyed a meal of kibbles and table scraps at her residence before being lead by her owner for a walk in the park. Passersby testified to hearing strange "popping sounds" emitting from the dogs posterior area followed by foul odors. "It made my eyes water," alleged one witness. "That dog waited for me to walk past before pulling the trigger. I swear she did it on purpose."

NAME: LULA
HEIGHT: 16"
WEIGHT: 23 LBS.

CHARGE: CROSSING STATE LINES
WITH A MINOR

Class II felony

The Benson family traveled from Rockford, Illinois to Ames, Iowa to visit the Sunnyhill bulldog Puppy Farm. Shortly after their arrival, daughter Amanda was introduced to and quickly fell in love with eight-week-old Lula. The happy couple then traveled together to Rockford aided and abetted by Rick and Shirley Benson, Amanda's parents, and have to this date avoided prosecution.

NAME: BOBO
HEIGHT: 22"
WEIGHT: 67 LBS.

CHARGE: SHOPLIFTING
Class III felony

Bobo accompanied his master into the local pet shop.
Despite leash restraint, he nevertheless managed to
quickly gain access to the store countertop and eat two
dog biscuits from a bowl on open display. The wayward
dog was arrested on the spot. Bobo's embarrassed owner
paid for the stolen property, leashed the dog outside,
and continued shopping without further incident.
Charges were subsequently dropped.

NAME: TINA
HEIGHT: 26"
WEIGHT: 88 LBS.

CHARGE: UNBEARABLE HAUGHTINESS
Class III misdemeanor

Tina's personal history was that of a well-behaved and friendly bulldog. Since being fitted with a jewel-encrusted tiara, however, her attitude has allegedly changed markedly. "She's acting like a snotty little princess," claims owner Marjorie Simpson.

NAME: SADIE
HEIGHT: 16"
WEIGHT: 25 LBS.

CHARGE: UNCOOPERATIVE BEHAVIOR
Class III misdemeanor

Apparently morose at being left behind while the rest of the family visited Six Flags Amusement Park over the weekend, dog-sitting security guards described Sadie as listless, without appetite and generally uncooperative. Authorities recommend her release on Monday morning.

NAME: HARLEY
HEIGHT: 24"
WEIGHT: 77 LBS.

CHARGE: PUBLIC NUISANCE: PEEPING TOM
Class II misdemeanor

Authorities responding to a neighborhood complaint of a peeping Tom observed a three-year-old bulldog identified as Harley staring at them from a nearby picket fence. "Downright unnerving" one official was reported as saying. Suspect fled as authorities approached and a house to house search was underway.

NAME: MAURICE
HEIGHT: 27"
WEIGHT: 109 LBS.

CHARGE: LEWD & LACIVIOUS BEHAVIOR
(SIXTH OFFENSE)

Class II misdemeanor

Maurice, age eleven years, is described by some witnesses
as "a dirty old bulldog"; by others as "an incurable
romantic." In either light and despite his advanced age,
Maurice chronically approaches female dogs of all breeds
in assertive attempts to mate. Although continually
rebuffed, Maurice remains shamelessly persistent, or
as one local official observed, "That dog can still hunt."

NAME: PETE
HEIGHT: 20"
WEIGHT: 69 LBS.

CHARGE: RESISTING ARREST
Class III felony

During the daily walk with his owners, Pete was suddenly accosted by a yipping, unleashed chihuahua. The outraged bulldog managed to break free from his owners and chase the offending chihuahua for half a block before finally being restrained. Charges against Pete were dropped when it was deemed that the dog was acting in his own self defense.

NAME: ANNIE
HEIGHT: 28"
WEIGHT: 96 LBS.

CHARGE: SPEEDING
Class I misdemeanor

Witnesses report that Annie, a two-year-old bulldog with a history of raucous behavior, was observed appropriating and operating a skateboard owned by neighborhood juvenile, Lyle Cooper. The perp was pursued by her owner down a driveway and into the street where she forced a vehicle to a screeching stop. Despite her subsequent arrest and punishment, it is suspected that this is not the last entry on Annie's already lengthy rap sheet.

NAME: LILY
HEIGHT: 15"
WEIGHT: 23 LBS.

CHARGE: DISTURBING THE PEACE
Class III misdemeanor

A six-week-old recently weaned bulldog puppy, aka Lily, was welcomed to the home of her new owners, Matt and Natalie Wilson, with the expectation that she would be a happy member of an otherwise quiet household. To the dismay of Matt and Natalie, the puppy howled for three consecutive nights. The Wilson's refused to file charges after investigators determined Lily's wailing resulted from her anguish over leaving her mother and littermates. Lily has been placed on parole.

NAME: SCOOTER
HEIGHT: 16"
WEIGHT: 30 LBS.

CHARGE: DEFYING AUTHORITY
Class I misdemeanor

Scooter is a six-week-old white American bulldog and the most raucous and rebellious member of a five puppy litter. Finally exasperated at Scooter's chronic unruly behavior, his mother singled him out for a growling scolding. Her actions terrified Scooter's littermates, but the offender stood his ground and remained unrepentant. Authorities have deemed the puppy incorrigible.

NAME: TOOTSIE
HEIGHT: 30"
WEIGHT: 113 LBS.

CHARGE: PUBLIC NUISANCE: PANHANDLING
Class III misdemeanor

Roaming without a leash in a public park, Tootsie was
observed approaching passersby and aggressively
begging for handouts. She had disappeared by the
time authorities responded to complaints. The incident
remains under investigation.

NAME: CARLO
HEIGHT: 18"
WEIGHT: 24 LBS.

CHARGE: WILLFUL DISOBEDIENCE
Class III misdemeanor

Although semi-house trained, Carlo was placed behind bars when the seven-week-old bulldog piddled on the living room rug three times during the course of a two hour period. Carlo was so overjoyed upon his release one-half hour later that he immediately peed in the kitchen.

NAME: DOLLY
HEIGHT: 26"
WEIGHT: 98 LBS.

CHARGE: PETTY THEFT
Class I misdemeanor

The facts in this case are clear: there are two plastic chew bones in the Adams' household, one for Dolly; one for Coco. Not satisfied with this arrangement, Dolly hides her bone and swipes Coco's acting as if it were her own. A search of the household for evidence of Dolly's bone is underway before charges can be filed.

NAME: MILLY
HEIGHT: 26"
WEIGHT: 102 LBS.

CHARGE: FAILURE TO SHARE
Class III misdemeanor

Milly and Copper are two bulldogs residing at 712 E.
Beaumont Avenue. Complaint indicates that Milly will not
allow cohabitation of the comfy dog pillow in the den
and has repeatedly threatened plaintiff with low growls
and bared teeth upon his approach to said pillow.
Authorities suggest temporary separation and counseling.

NAME: ROSEY
HEIGHT: 29"
WEIGHT: 117 LBS.

CHARGE: SOLICITING
Class II felony

Rosey is a four-year-old bulldog currently in heat.
Complaints site that Rosey has recently been trolling
the neighborhood in search of likely suitors, sometimes
boldly appearing at the doorsteps of homes of local male
dogs. She has since been apprehended and sentenced to
two weeks of home confinement.

CHARGE: ATTEMPTED ESCAPE
Class I misdemeanor

Duke and Jack are two bulldogs with a known record for leaving the yard. Temporarily incarcerated in an outside pen for the benefit of fresh air, the suspects burrowed beneath, pushed against, and climbed the bars in continued attempts to escape. Exasperated officials returned them to home confinement where charges are pending.

NAME: OSCAR
HEIGHT: 25"
WEIGHT: 92 LBS.

CHARGE: PHILANDERING
Class I misdemeanor

Oscar has become a neighborhood nuisance and blatant philanderer. Subject is routinely released from house arrest under the pretext of doing his duty only to furtively slip from sight. While his master issues the "Come" command, Oscar is roaming the neighborhood for winsome females including Yorkies, chihuahuas, dachshunds, and once, incredibly, a Labrador retriever.

NAME: RICCO
HEIGHT: 27"
WEIGHT: 106 LBS.

CHARGE: ORGANIZED CRIME BOSS
Class II felony

Ricco (aka "Dogfather") is a nine-year-old bulldog convicted of being the acting Crime Boss of the Lafredo Family. The eldest of three dogs in the Lafredo household, Ricco had eluded arrest for such crimes as piddling on the kitchen floor, chewed furniture, and stolen dog biscuits. Instead, his younger gang members, Lefty and Tony, had taken the fall. That all changed following a recent sting operation in which authorities employed a web cam to catch Ricco in various criminal acts while his gang looked on. The court will take into consideration the dog's advanced age before sentencing.

NAME: PONGO
HEIGHT: 30"
WEIGHT: 112 LBS.

CHARGE: POSSESSION OF STOLEN PROPERTY: HIDING EVIDENCE

Class II misdemeanor

Authorities were alerted by an all-points-bulletin directing them to the kitchen where Pongo was discovered with the contents of a box of dog biscuits he had managed to snatch from the counter. As authorities closed in, Pongo began devouring the evidence but not enough to prevent his speedy arrest and conviction.

NAME: KANA
HEIGHT: 16"
WEIGHT: 20 LBS.

CHARGE: DESTRUCTION OF
PRIVATE PROPERTY

Class III felony

A shocking string of heinous crimes has rattled dismayed householders in the Edgewood Avenue neighborhood who alerted authorities to widespread damage to their flower gardens. The ensuing investigation lead to a stunning revelation: The havoc was caused by just one little bulldog puppy, aka Kana, whose owners took full responsibility for damages caused by the juvenile delinquent. The perpetrator remains incarcerated in her yard by a newly installed Invisible Fence.

NAME: NETTIE
HEIGHT: 23"
WEIGHT: 74 LBS.

CHARGE: INGESTING A FOUL SUBSTANCE
Class III misdemeanor

Repeat offender Nettie is a three-year-old bulldog with a history of surreptitiously consuming banned substances while foraging in the backyard. This alone and of itself is a canine misdemeanor, but charges are increased to second degree felony when said substances are habitually retched within the household.